MW01384381

A Pocket Full of Resilience

Inspiration on How to Accept, Overcome, and Grow from the Suffering in Your Life

Waleuska Lazo

DreamCatcher Print

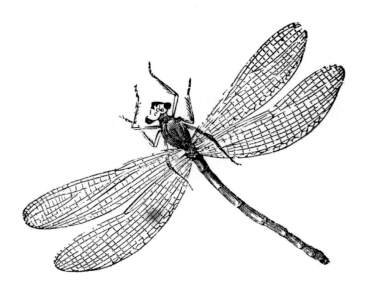

ABOUT THIS BOOK

Resilience is a powerful skill worth developing. Like strengthening any muscle in your body, the more you strengthen your resilience, the more adaptive you will be to things that are beyond your control. Resilience is not only about being able to withstand and recover quickly from difficult situations, but also learning from them so that you can plan, respond, accept, overcome, recover, thrive, and even feel joyful based on what you learn and discover despite the realities of our changing world.

May this book infuse you with relief, resilience, wisdom, and hope. Use this book when you are feeling stressed or lost and in need of guidance and encouragement. Each message was created with the energy of the divine. Before you open the book, close your eyes and set an intention to receive the message that is meant for you in the moment by opening it (or scrolling) to a random page. The page will reveal the message you are meant to hear.

In this book, I will use the words *God, Life,* and *the Universe* interchangeably to mean a divine cosmic power. It is my hope you get to love this book as much as I loved writing it for you.

Waleuska Lazo

Nobody gets to their destiny without a few scars.

There are emotional hurts that mark us for life, hurts that cut deeply into our souls, leaving scars as evidence. These are the scars of betrayal, loss, divorce, financial failure, and regretting things we wish had been different.

If you're struggling right now with any of these hurts and you are trying to hide or deny them because you cannot see anything good in them, you may be blocking your ability to heal and evolve as a person.

BE PROUD OF YOUR SCARS.

Learn to honor them, NOT as things you had to endure, but as things you SURVIVED.

Your mind is a garden and you are its landscaper. You can harvest beauty or weeds. Seed it carefully.

Stay hopeful! Your deepest hurt might be a blessing in disguise.

I've learned that just as some rocks are diamonds in disguise, our hurts can be blessings in disguise. Just as it takes extreme heat and pressure beneath the earth for rocks to transform into beautiful gems, it can also take grief, disappointment, and heartbreak for us to learn, transform, and evolve.

Pain has a hidden purpose.

The Universe puts us in difficult situations so we can learn to be resilient, not so we can struggle. For it is in dark moments of affliction that we discover how genuinely strong we are. The strength that is born from pain is a source of incredible resilience.

When you see how much you've pulled yourself through, you can look back and be proud.

Sit with the sadness. Acknowledge it.

Don't try to drink or medicate your sorrow away. Running, sleeping, or eating to suppress and avoid your sorrow won't make it disappear. Sadness and regret can only be healed by feeling what you feel.

Your mind will believe everything you tell it.

The person you are and the life you have are the result of your beliefs and habits. Therefore, if you wish to upgrade the quality of your life, you must upgrade the quality of the thoughts you think.

It is not necessarily those who have the most that are happy. It is those who enjoy what they have that are happiest.

It is difficult to define happiness because happiness is subjective. What makes someone happy may not be what makes another happy. But it is safe to say that those who live with contentment and gratitude in their hearts are the happiest.

When you can't find a solution to a problem, it's a cue that there is something you need to accept.

When confronted with undesirable situations, our natural tendency is to respond negatively and fight the outcome even when we know we cannot control it. For example, getting frustrated because there is construction on the road on your way to work is not going to make the traffic move faster. Accepting that there is a delay, however, will go a long way toward preserving your mental health.

Acceptance is a powerful tool. Focus on how to respond best to the unpleasant or unexpected circumstances that Life throws your way and you'll be able to respond with calmness and grace.

The secret to being happy is in finding beauty in simple things.

Life is not just about the monumental moments. It is not about winning the Super Bowl, or World Cup-level achievements. It is about the ordinary things, such as waking up and feeling the warmth of the person you love lying by your side. It is about enjoying simple comforts like taking a cool shower on a hot day, electricity to illuminate your house at night, or having a car to drive around in. Happiness is about being grateful that the sun came out today, or even better, that your head left the pillow this morning because it means you are alive.

Thank Life for what she puts in your way, what she takes away, and what she accommodates.

Worrying and stressing doesn't make things better. Believing that everything is somehow happening for your greatest good, however, even in moments when you cannot yet see how, may help you see your life from a more resilient angle. The Universe has a way of accommodating our needs, so give it a chance to unravel the knots and work things out for you.

Thank Life for the doors that close, as well as for those that open. Once the old is gone, you have room for the new. Trust that the Universe knows why different things are happening in your life.

How you feel is not as much about what happens to you as how you interpret what happens.

Your brain receives all sorts of data through your senses, but it doesn't always know how to interpret it. It relies on you to give the data meaning.

Events that produce an emotional charge make the brain release chemicals into your body to match the emotion you are feeling. If a new experience reminds you of a past experience when you felt fear, anger, sadness, or grief, your brain will match your current chemistry to those feelings. The only way to build resilience is by consciously changing the interpretation you give to the current events.

It is not events or people that make an impact on our biology; it is the meaning we assign to them. So, the next time you're feeling challenged, change the way you interpret what's going on. Instead of deciding that you're confronting something bad which is here to hurt you, do your best to see it as happening to teach you something.

Sometimes a shift in thinking is all that's needed to fix a problem.

The quality of your life improves in direct proportion to how you respond internally to whatever you experience. Your interpretations will either help you accept and overcome unpleasant events or leave you feeling victimized by them.

The next time you face a challenge, ask yourself, "What is this experience trying to teach me? What gift might I derive from it?" If you change how you approach your difficulties to this, you'll begin to build emotional resilience.

Never let the conditions of your outer world dictate your inner being because this is the essence of you.

Nine simple things that can help you live more resiliently.

1. Upon waking, spend five minutes each morning expressing profound gratitude for Life.

2. Start your day by drinking a glass of water.

3. Squeeze the juice of half a lime into a glass, put a pinch of salt into it, and then drink it as you would a shot.

4. Exercise. Do whatever you can, but move.

5. Supplement your diet with magnesium, vitamins D and C, and probiotics.

6. Eliminate sugar and refined carbohydrates from your diet.

7. Eat less often. Intermittent fasting helps us live longer and healthier.

8. Spend time with your family doing stuff you love.

9. Go to bed early and aim to get a minimum of eight hours of sleep a night.

The most profound moments in your life often come when you find the courage to stop trying to change that which can't be changed.

We can't make people love us any more than we can part the waters of the ocean. Still, it can be heart-wrenching when someone leaves us. Sometimes the more we try to hold on, the faster they go, and wanting to know why can be excruciating.

That is, until the moment we realize that it is not for us to know. Not for us to change the outcome. It is at this moment of recognition that we are set free. Surrendering control can be the path to peace.

You can only heal what you allow yourself to feel.

Many people don't understand that we carry our emotional and psychological trauma in the cells and organs of our bodies. Just because we pretend they aren't there does not mean they are gone. They live in our bodies, waiting for something to happen to free them. If they're suppressed, they can manifest as all sorts of different illnesses.

Let yourself:

- Feel.
- Cry.
- Breathe.
- Accept.
- Release.

You have two choices: You can be embittered by what Life throws at you or you can use it to make you a better, stronger, wiser person.

Our power resides in how we choose to respond. Even the most unwanted things hold lessons for us. But we may have to dig to discover them.

The next time you find yourself having a hard time seeing any purpose for what has happened, say to yourself, "I don't see the purpose here yet. I don't understand the plan. But I believe something useful will come out of this situation."

By learning to mine for purpose, you can overcome anything and will feel much less resentful. Try it!

You never know... What initially may seem like a detour from your dreams might actually be the most direct route to having your dreams come true. Stay calm. Keep the faith. Trust the Universe.

You'll never get to fully express yourself if you keep hiding from the very things in life that prepare you to meet your destiny.

Any time you pretend, hide, shame, or deny a painful part of your life, you deny your humanity. Everything you feel—including hurt, love, joy, and loss—is part of what makes you special, skillful, and strong. In fact, the very things you may be trying to avoid showing could be exactly what is needed so that you can grow into what you were born to inevitably do.

When you focus on trying to be what you are not, you miss out on seeing the gift you really are.

Stop comparing yourself to others. Every person has a unique set of abilities and talents. But if you spend your time wishing to be like others or have what they have, then you will never feel you're enough.

If you constantly focus on a quality or virtue you think you lack, you may fail to use your gifts at all and rob the world of them. Instead, look at what you have and who you are, and build on it.

Thinking of all the things you *don't* want wills them into existence.

Most people spend more time thinking about the things they don't want than what they do want. They don't realize that thoughts are beacons of energy powerful enough to pull things, people, and circumstances to you. Anything that resonates with the frequency of your thoughts is drawn in. So, be mindful of where your mental energy is going because you may inadvertently attract something you wish to avoid.

Remember, you attract what you think about on a consistent basis. If you focus on what you want and you do it in a grateful way, thanking the Universe in advance for those things before they manifest, you will attract more things to be thankful for.

The only thing that comes at us out of an empty sky is rain. If you want a successful life, you must plan for it and follow through every day with action.

Get in the habit of setting goals. Make monthly and yearly goals, and map out how to get where you want to be and accomplish what you want to have accomplished one, five, and ten years down the road. Something amazing begins to happen when you do this. Because your mind is clear, it will go to work finding you the resources, people, and opportunities necessary to meet your goals.

You know you are evolving when you begin to take responsibility for the life you've created.

It is easier to look for something or someone to blame for the things that happen to us. Rarely do we look inward and take personal responsibility for our lives in their entirety. We blame how we feel on the weather, on our jobs, our upbringings, on the state of the world, and on the behavior of the people around us, not realizing that we are emitting an energy that attracts experiences that resonate with it. Once you take responsibility for your energy and what it attracts, you will become more skillful with your actions, thoughts, and decisions.

You are biologically resilient. Your body knows how to heal itself.

If you aren't feeling well, consider whether your mind could be making you sick. Your limiting beliefs, a narrative you feed your soul, and the emotions you feel as result of them could make you unwell and also prevent you from healing.

We are taught to look for healing agents outside of ourselves. We look to people and circumstances to make us whole, but true healing comes from within. The natural state of our bodies is one of harmony, balance, peace, and health.

Your body always strives to restore its homeostasis. It is your job to create conditions that are right for it to heal. Each time you focus on seeking something external to make you whole and happy, you divert the energy that your body needs to use internally.

Whenever you find yourself being stressed, pause. Ask, "Is this worry worth my health?"

Depression doesn't discriminate. Privileged and underprivileged people are hit the same by it.

Depression attacks without discrimination. Even those who may seem to have it all can suffer from terrible depression and anxiety. You can never know the battles being fought behind closed doors. Be kind, mindful, and compassionate with everyone you meet and lift them up. It is possible that a kind word and gesture from you can help save a life. You can improve the resilience of the people you meet.

Memorize three magic phrases: I love you. I am proud of you. I accept you.

There is a simple way to make a lasting difference in someone's life that doesn't require you to buy them lavish gifts or spend any money. Tell them that they are loved, you are proud of them, and you accept them for who they are. These words plant seeds of hope and resilience in the mind of whomever hears them.

Great adversity can give us a great sense of purpose.

Painful circumstances often prepare us to play an extraordinary role in life because they reveal what needs to be addressed and healed. They also show us how to overcome challenges, so we can teach others.

The most admirable people typically have survived great adversity. They then found a way to use their pain and misfortune as tools for motivation, growth, and service. We can do the same!

It's not that life is short.
It's that we waste so much of it.

You are granted 1,440 precious minutes a day. This may seem to be a lot of time, but it is like the blink of an eye. Once gone, a day can't be recovered.

If you're wasteful about how you spend your time, before you know it, your life will have passed you by. At the end, you'll think it was too short.

Time can't be stopped, banked, stored, refunded, or replaced. So, be mindful of how you are spending those 1,440 minutes. Are you spending them in joy or in stress? With loved ones or alone?

Make each day count.

A life worth living requires you to:

- Get up grateful to see a new a day.
- Give thanks for what you have.
- Do something productive and something fun each day.
- Do something to help someone else.
- Nurture your body and soul.
- Exercise.
- Say "I love you" to someone.
- Do something that pushes you out of your comfort zone.
- Learn something new.

BE GRATEFUL for all things that end. What is meant for you will flow to you. What is not meant for you will wither away. Let it!

Learn to look at everything in your life not as bad or good, but as a learning opportunity either to do better or be better and evolve. Sometimes we hold on to a job or a relationship for far too long. We stubbornly see its ending as a failure or a loss. But in fact, by prolonging a necessary ending, we block what is meant for us from arriving in our lives.

Breathe . . .

YOU'VE GOT THIS!

The Universe gives you only what you need.

The Universe will use any means necessary to get your attention and awaken you. People, especially those with whom we are the most intimate, serve as mirrors to reflect what is hidden in the depths of our souls from ourselves, so we can see it. When the Universe feels we are ready, it will bring us mirrors to help us heal what needs to be healed.

Sometimes the person you want most to be with is a person you would be better off without.

Just because some things were meant to happen does not mean your relationship was meant to be.

Just because someone came into your life does not mean they are meant to stay forever. If their journey with you feels too short, remember that it may still have been long enough to teach you something valuable.

Being happier each day is just one adjustment away. If you wish to improve your mental state, start by shifting your attention to things that are going right.

The idea of someone coming to complete you is damaging.

No person that comes into your life is able to make you whole or make you feel loved and validated. That is just a fantasy you learned from the romantic movies you watch. The phrase "You complete me" in the Tom Cruise movie *Jerry Maguire* (1996) did a disfavor to many people. The truth is that even in the absence of a relationship, you are already WHOLE. You are already COMPLETE.

No one can repeatedly betray you without you betraying yourself.

Whether or not we like to admit it, consciously or not, there are always signs that we can pick up on beforehand of someone betraying us. If you need to risk any of your core values to stay connected to someone, then you are already betraying yourself. Any relationship that requires you to change who you are or to compromise any part of you is not a conscious, loving, responsible relationship. Learn to acknowledge the signs. They are always there.

When your passion is aligned with what you do, the Universe conspires to help you succeed. Why? Because you are doing what you were born to do!

Find your WHY to live.

To live a fulfilled life, you need to find a reason to live for. Discover what you love to do and do that each day of your life. Make that your WHY.

Too many people work at jobs they hate and dread. Find what makes you want to get up in the morning and figure out a way to monetize it so you can make a life doing what you love, as well as a living.

A key to resilience is loving what you have and nurturing it.

The formula to having a peaceful, joyful life is so simple that many of us dismiss it. It seems that we can't reconcile how something so simple can be the answer to our endless quest for happiness. But it is.

We all have the wick of a happy life buried inside of us. Gratitude for what you already have is the spark that ignites this wick and lights up the feeling of happiness we have been searching for everywhere.

Happiness is not something you can touch, hold, or acquire because it is already within you.

Three powerful questions to ask yourself each morning are:

- What am I grateful for?
- How can I be of service?
- Who do I choose to be when I leave this bed?

If you try to escape heartbreak, you may also sacrifice the feeling of love. To love with your heart open is to risk losses. There can always be the possibility of hurt that often comes from loving someone deeply. But this is part of the human experience. You must decide if you are brave enough. Try it. It is worth the risk every time!

Take chances.
Leap into the unknown.

When you are on your deathbed looking back over your life, how would you like to remember it? Would you rather say, "I am so glad I did that" or "I wish I had done that"?

There is no right or wrong option here. Whichever one you choose is fine. This is your story, your journey. Just make sure you choose now so you can live your life accordingly and prevent regrets.

You can choose to look down at the mud or up at the stars.

Life is all about choices and your state of being is their consequence. You can choose to focus on all that is wrong in the world or you can choose to focus on what is right and find lessons everywhere you look. Your quality of life is strongly dependent on the level of perspective you give to things.

Thank you, beloved Universe, for the doors you closed in my face. Thank you for not allowing me to settle for second best. Thank you for showing me that the "no" I heard was said for my protection.

Do something today that takes you outside your comfort zone.

Biologically, for your survival, you were made to be a creature of habit. Keeping safe by taking the path of least resistance is what your brain likes. However, if your goal is to grow, evolve, and achieve more, then you must push beyond the boundaries of your fear. Each day before you go to bed, ask yourself, *"Did I face my fears today? Did I try something new? Did I do something different?"*

To feel rich, count the blessings you have that money can't buy.

Remember to do this the next time you catch yourself feeling deprived or limited.

- If you woke up this morning,
- If you can see,
- If you can hear,
- If you have health,
- If you can walk,
- If someone loves you,
- If you love someone,
- If you have friends you can trust,
- If you have family to lean on,
- If you have purpose in your life . . .

Then, you are richer than you realize.

Painful events can teach us things we didn't even know we needed to learn.

At some point in your life, you will be presented with a situation that shakes you, something you would rather not experience. Yet, there you are. Do yourself a favor and see what you can learn about yourself from whatever is happening. Use it as a launchpad to get to the next level of wisdom. Assume that Life is your teacher.

Close this book right now and do something kind for yourself.

Life is like gelato. Savor it.

Walking through the streets in Florence, Italy, I noticed a gelato shop on every street. Although there were many, none was empty. The people took time to delight in the many flavors. Not being able to help myself, I said out loud to an elderly man in line, "Wow, Italians do love gelato!"

He smiled and responded, "For us, gelato is a way of life. It's a reminder to stop and delight in the moment. There is no point living this long and not enjoying the pleasures of Life."

Point taken! Life, like gelato, is not meant just to be on display. It is meant to be savored. Like the many gelato flavors, Life too offers us many experiences, some we will like more than others, but in the end, we must embrace them before they melt away!

Refrain from making predictions, especially those that make you feel anxious.

You are not a fortune teller, so things you spend time worrying about may never happen. Eliminate fear of the future and watch your stress diminish.

To be happy, learn to embrace the unknown as a place where all possibilities exist. Feel excitement (rather than fear) over what is yet to come.

Let go of the past.

Use the past as a guide and a teacher, but do not ruminate on it or you will risk recreating what you want to avoid.

The only way out of your pain is going THROUGH it.

The law of manifestation is about vibration.

Nothing can be manifested that does not match or resonate with the frequencies of our thoughts and emotions. Therefore, if you are unhappy with your life, you must look at the energy you are emitting. Is it loving and positive or fearful and negative?

Too many people spend more energy thinking about things they DON'T want than they do thinking about things they DO want. Inadvertently, they end up bringing what they wish to avoid into existence.

Given how manifestation works, the question you need to ask yourself is: *Am I fueling my fears or am I fueling my dreams?*

If you feel stressed, notice if your expectations match your reality.

It is you (and you alone) who creates your stress and disappointment. Yes, people may hurt you and things may unexpectedly come up to disturb the natural rhythm of your life, but for the most part, it is the gap between your expectations about how things should be and how things actually are that will cause you to feel dissatisfied.

Zero expectation leads to zero suffering.

When in doubt,
listen to your heart.

Getting your shit together may require a level of honest self-scrutiny from you that hurts.

Until you take responsibility for what you have created, you cannot make your life better. Yes, there are many things you cannot control, but there are also many things you can. The next time you look in the mirror, have a heart-to-heart talk with your reflection. If you don't like what you see, you have some work to do to change your world.

Struggle teaches us how to fly.

Don't be so quick to complain about your struggles. An eaglet only discovers how to use its wings after it has fallen out of the nest and is fighting not to hit the ground. As it flaps its wings, it discovers how to fly. You have natural abilities that can keep you aloft in your life. Learn to feel grateful for each moment of struggle as it is there to help you learn to fly.

Hitting rock bottom may be the best thing that happens to you.

Sometimes hitting rock bottom is what we need to do before we can change. Transformation seldom arises from glory. It is usually born when we're in the depths of despair.

If you find yourself at a low point right now, be grateful. This is the Universe knocking on your soul's door. It is your call to be brave and let parts of you that don't serve your highest good die.

Life didn't promise you'd have days without pain and sorrow. Instead, it promised you strength to overcome and light to guide you out of darkness.

It is all right to feel sad after making a tough decision.

Making tough decisions isn't easy. It takes courage to decide what is right for you and stand by it. Feelings of loss and grief might make you question your instincts and judgment. Though it is normal to feel "buyer's remorse," this doesn't mean that your decision wasn't the correct one. Stay on course.

Don't give up. You may be closer to your goal than you realize.

When you feel like you have exhausted every avenue, climbed every mountain, walked every mile, this is the time when you must persevere.

In *Og Mandino's University of Success,* Mandino tells a dramatic story about the discovery in 1942 of one of the biggest diamonds in history, called the Liberator, which was sold for what would be the equivalent of almost four million dollars today.

Rafael Solano had been mining for diamonds in a dry riverbed in Venezuela with two other men for months with no success. Feeling exhausted and discouraged, he said, "I quit. This must be the 999, 999th pebble I've picked up and not one was a diamond. There is no use in continuing to search."

"Well, pick up one more and make it an even million, then we can go home," said his friend.

Solano stooped one more time and . . . yes, you guessed correctly . . . that millionth pebble was the purest and biggest diamond ever found.

When all else fails, persist. If this is only your 999,999th try, make it a million! You could be only one step away from your Liberator!

It does not matter what the day is like. What makes the day beautiful is YOU!

How you feel about your day today is up to you. Happiness is something we decide ahead of time. Regardless of what is happening around us, we get to decide how we respond.

If your day seems to be tanking, breathe through the challenges and keep a positive perspective. Nothing is permanent and this too shall pass.

Being a spiritual person doesn't shield you from pain. Spirituality makes you resilient so that you can endure and survive pain.

It is sometimes thought that being spiritual or having faith in God/the Universe/Life can make us immune to pain. That, if we pray and do rituals that prove we believe, we can avoid at least some of the suffering in life. But this is not the case. Bad things happen to good people and spiritual people too.

Where the resilience comes from is the belief that all which you experience, whether good or bad, has a purpose. This lessens suffering. The idea that there is an invisible force guiding you so that you may learn, is more powerful than anything Life can throw at you.

Use "I am" statements to send a powerful, divine manifestation frequency out into the Universe.

Go to a mirror, look at yourself, and say:

- I am strong.
- I am whole.
- I am enough.
- I am protected.
- I am resilient.
- I am worthy.
- I am healthy.
- I am at peace.
- I am blessed.
- I am joy.
- I am abundant.

Miracles happen when you give energy to your dreams.

Only one emotion can prevail at any given time. So, spend energy feeding your dreams. Each time you catch yourself thinking about something else that takes you away from the uplifting frequency of your dreams, interrupt yourself. Speak to yourself out loud if you must, to overcome this digression!

Each interruption is a victory, a way to program your subconscious mind to create your desires.

It's never too late to embark on a new journey, write a new story, or build a new dream for yourself.

Just because something else didn't pan out doesn't mean it's the end for you. There is nothing stopping you from setting sail for a new horizon. That is a beautiful part of Life. It offers us the opportunity to start over each day when the sun rises.

If you can breathe, you can dream. And if you can dream it, you can achieve it.

Accept what Life takes away from you with graciousness, having complete faith that the Universe is only removing it to make room for what is actually yours.

Success of any kind is achieved through consistency.

I don't know of any achievement that is accomplished without consistent effort. Success, be it in a relationship, in business, or in cultivating personal mastery of any kind, requires diligence. When you apply effort consistently to an endeavor, the cumulative impact of taking even small daily actions can propel you to great achievement.

When you practice being consistent, your self-discipline will lead you to develop and master other worthy habits that, in turn, help you attain goals. So, devise a routine that is congruent with your goals and follow through with consistency.

Decide what you want for your life and say no to anything that isn't it.

Achievement of a dream is simpler than most people know; but it is not easy for those who are undisciplined about adhering to their vision.

The first thing you need to do is to become crystal clear on what you want your life to be like.

Then you must take the actions, create the habits, and follow with consistency to do the things that take you closer each day towards living that life. Say no to anything that doesn't resemble the life you want or push you closer to getting what you want. Everything else needs to be eliminated from your daily actions.

If you don't like what you see, BE the change!

Chronic complaining is a disease in our society. It is easier to whine and lament than to be responsible. But if you don't like something, you can do something about it. The world only changes when someone stops complaining and takes action.

If you are not prepared to get involved and put in the work to solve problems, then say nothing.

The most inspiring person is the one who overcomes their fear.

Many people think being courageous means not being afraid. This cannot be further from the truth. Courage cannot exist in the absence of fear.

Do you want to be an inspiring person? Then embrace your fear and move ahead with your plans anyhow. We don't admire those who have no fear. What is so courageous about that? We admire those who feel vulnerable and yet make progress every day. We admire those brave people who are heartbroken yet take the risk to love again.

You can only go as far as you believe you're worthy of going.

Train your mind to see goodness everywhere.

When your brain gets excited about something, it brings it into focus and, through selective attention, filters out everything unrelated to that thing. Your brain views the emotional charge as meaningful.

If you practice noticing goodness, your brain says, "Ah, you are expressing an interest in goodness, so I am going to help by looking for more goodness."

Hardships reveal hidden treasures.

Rainbows appear in the sky after rainstorms. Diamonds are made from friction. Our strengths emerge when Life puts pressure on us.

Difficult moments you would rather avoid may be the ones you need to lean into the most.

As difficult as handling some moments may be, if you are constantly trying to bypass discomfort, pain, and grief, you may also be bypassing the very things that can help you evolve.

Important lessons to remember:

- Just because something ended doesn't mean it failed.

- Not every relationship is meant to go the distance.

- Patience is an existential tool.

- Express what you really feel and want. People cannot read your mind.

- Forgive mistakes quickly.

- Make up with the people you love.

- Short-term memory is an asset when it comes to arguing with people you love.

- You attract what you consistently think about.

- Believe in miracles, as they do happen.

- The grass is never greener on the other side.

- Listen wholeheartedly.

- Assume the good always.

- Be someone else's safe haven.

- Be honest even if it's difficult.

- Things are never as bad as you make them out to be.

- Don't assume you'll have time for things later. Do them now!

You will only see divine signs when you are ready to act on them.

A divine force is in constant communication with you, sending you signs to guide you through your life. Unfortunately, until you are ready to act on the signs, they won't register in your mind. Sometimes a sign will come in the form of a coincidence or serendipity, other times it will come in the form of a painful event. All signs are designed to awaken you and guide you to your ultimate destiny.

Once you're ready, the signs the Universe is sending will become apparent to you. Watch for them!

On the path to your dreams, fear will always be there to meet you.

As we get closer to attaining our goals, more fear will appear to erect a wall in front of us. This is where most people stop because they don't realize that fear's role is not to stop them. Fear is actually there to invite you to pause so you may learn, investigate, and prepare further. It is never intended to push you permanently off the path to your dreams.

If you are meeting difficulties on your path, they could mean you are closer than you think to your goals. Knowing that fear is showing up to test you and see how committed you are to your dreams, your role is to listen to fear, respect it for what it is trying to inform you about, make accommodations if needed, then keep moving ahead with your plan.

To feel better about your life, do something kind for someone else.

The most fragile thing in the world is trust. Once broken, it never repairs.

Trust is our most valuable currency in relationships. Without it, we have nothing. It is also delicate. If we are fortunate to enjoy trust, we must be mindful not to damage it. Once this bond is broken, even with the best efforts and intention to put it back together, a relationship is never quite the same. In spite of our best efforts, there is always a voice that whispers, "But can I trust this person again?" The uncertainty caused by the possibility of a repeated hurt never truly goes away.

You can have tremendous love for a person, but your trust may be more powerful and important. Without it, the love may not be enough to stay connected. You will always love a person you trust, but you may not always trust a person you love.

Be mindful of never damaging this delicate gem. If you are fortunate to have people you can trust who trust you, you may consider yourself blessed.

Things happen in perfect timing even if it's not the timing you like.

Yes. Everything comes in perfect timing. Sometimes that timing will seem like a blessing, a source of joy. In some situations, the timing hits you like lightning. You may be struck at your core by the timing of something that occurs and hate being surprised. Whichever way timing happens, rest assured that it is happening because it is what is necessary at the moment to prepare you for or carry you to your ultimate destiny.

It is impossible to see any purpose in the Universe's plans in moments when you are reeling. But when you give Life enough time, it will reveal its purpose. Until you can see the plan clearly, you just have to sit tight. Endure the storm of events at your door and know that it is in your ability to accept things with grace and gratitude that you will eventually see why, indeed, there is nothing but perfect timing.

Closure can come at unexpected times and in unexpected ways.

In moments when you are desperately seeking to understand the why of things and derive some meaning from them, you have three choices.

1. You can drive yourself crazy looking for a reason why and imagining all kinds of things that may have nothing to do with the actual reason.

2. You can stay bitter and let the experience define you.

3. You can accept what happens as real, and choose not to let it hold you hostage emotionally.

Don't be dependent on closure for happiness. Often, the more we chase after feelings, the more they evade us. If we let things be, the closure we are looking for can arrive out of the blue. Stay open!

Not every person you meet will like you. Be at peace with that.

Though it is natural to want to be liked, let go of the notion that you have to be liked by everyone you meet. This is unachievable, so wanting it will be counterproductive and set you up for disappointment. Instead, feel blessed on occasions when you are liked—and blessed when you are not. The Universe ultimately will clear those who aren't worthy of being part of your story from your path.

Here are some crazy statistics I heard reported by Joel Osteen in a podcast: 25 percent of the people you know don't like you, but 25 percent more could be persuaded to like you. Another 25 percent of the people you know like you presently, but could be persuaded not to. Fortunately, 25 percent will like you no matter what. Focus your energy on them!

Thank the Universe for ordinary moments.

Today, your call of action is to become mindful of and thankful for the small, ordinary moments that Life gifts you which please you.

I'll get you started with my own list.

- I laughed out loud.
- I looked up at the sun and let its rays warm my face.
- I went for a walk with my mother.
- I stayed up late with a friend and talked about our lives for hours.
- I did a kind act for a stranger.

What simple things are you grateful for?

Do you spend more time looking ahead or looking back?

Master the art of looking towards the life that is in front of you rather than the life that is behind you. Certainly, look to your past every so often as a point of reference and teaching tool, but never allow it to define you. Accept the losses, celebrate the wins, then focus all your attention on what is ahead.

If you are willing to have great failures and learn from them, you can end up achieving great things.

Every successful person who has achieved great things in their life knows that taking risks and failing are undeniable parts of the process. Failure and success go hand in hand because achievements are often built on the steps of our failures.

Thomas Edison is a great example of this principle. He loved failure! He's credited with saying: "Negative results are just what I want. They're just as valuable to me as positive results. I can never find the thing that does the job best, until I find the ones that don't." Edison apparently felt he wasn't succeeding *unless* he was failing.

When a reporter asked Edison how it felt to have failed so many times while creating the light bulb, he responded: "I have not failed. I've just found 10,000 ways that won't work."

Someday, soon, and tomorrow are days that don't exist in calendars.

Today is all you have. The present of the present moment is an overstated concept, yet one not fully embraced. Live today to your fullest. It is a privilege and a gift you are given. Don't postpone living, thinking tomorrow you will have time to do what you want to do and live through your adventures, because sadly, we all are living on borrowed time.

You are the hero of your story.

You are the main character of your own story. You are the writer and the protagonist, and you get to decide how your story goes. And like any other hero from legend, you will be tested. You will be given obstacles and challenges to overcome. There will be villains to contend with too. In such times, it is up to you to go forth and slay the dragons.

Remember, a story without a struggle is not a worthy story. So, the next time you are confronted with difficulties, remind yourself out loud, "I am not a victim. I am the HERO of my story!"

"The Universe never takes things away without compensating you for them by giving you something in return."

ROSA LAZO

Life is a succession of moments. Some are harsh, some perfect.

Life is what you make of it. It is realistic that Life will offer you highs and lows. Between middling days, you will occasionally enjoy a magical moment.

Some moments will be simple and profound. Some will be monumental and life changing. Your main job as an emotional being is to ride the waves of ups and downs with gratitude for all.

If you were to see an ECG scan of your heart, you would notice how the lines are never constant. They have peaks and valleys. Be grateful for those fluctuations because it means you are alive. The nature of Life is to fluctuate.

Be grateful for the darkness in your life because it forces you to build up your soul's "muscles."

The truth is that nobody gets strong without facing adversity, and despair causes us to grow the most. Adversity is the equivalent of lifting dumbbells at a gym. Doing multiple reps with heavy weights so as to stress the muscles enough to grow increases the mass and size of the muscles. When your muscle fibers sustain a minor injury or damage, this signals your body to repair the fibers by fusing them.

Challenges are the equivalent of weightlifting for the soul. The next time you find yourself going through something challenging, such as a loss or a lawsuit, you will be better able to endure it because the source of strength inside you is bigger now.

Sometimes what comes to you by coincidence actually makes you happier than the things you have fought so hard to keep.

Nothing is ever truly lost.

You never truly lose anyone or anything, although that is what it could seem like in the moment. You see, what is not in your best interest has a way of leaving you. People and things are on their own journeys, separate from yours. What is meant for your best and highest good has a way of coming back to you as your paths intersect again.

Not getting what you want can be a blessing.

Not getting your way can be a great blessing if you are willing to release your desire to control reality. Bitterness and pain make it difficult to see the hidden gifts of letting go of a hoped for plan. But letting go increases space in your head and heart.

Allow yourself to embrace the sadness or grief of a loss, and the discomfort you feel because of fighting the event. In so doing, you have the chance to realize that your thoughts and feelings are not you.

This gives you the power to choose how you are going to think, feel, and react to Life.

Know that you can overcome pain. Attach no meaning to it other than the significance of what it teaches. Follow the advice of your soul.

Sometimes, it's the smallest of decisions that changes a life.

Don't discount the power of small decisions. The cumulative effect of making good decisions can have a great impact on you. Think about this: If you didn't make the decision to brush your teeth every morning, most likely your gums would become infected after three months.

The decision to call a friend or smile at someone on the street, as easy as this gesture may be for you, can save a life if that person is in a state of crisis. Small decisions are critical building blocks of Life.

The path the Universe chooses for you may be greater than the one you've chosen for yourself.

When the Universe directs us to take a certain path that we don't understand, it is common to doubt it. Thinking we know better, we may end up following a different route. Especially if the path shown to us seems long and convoluted, we need to remember that the seemingly easier, shorter road we are contemplating taking could be full of dangerous narrow curves, bumpy stretches, and poorly lit dead-ends. Of course, there is no way for us to know that. Only the Universe does. Let's trust her!

You are on the right path. It may not seem like it at times, but stay the course. Your break is coming.

Grief can be as long lasting or as temporary as you allow it to be.

Everything passes. No matter how sad or anxious you feel right now or how unfortunate your loss is, there will be times when you experience happiness. Emotions, even grief, naturally flow and morph one into the next. None stays the same because Life is ever changing. But grief can feel permanent when you choose to dwell in the sorrow. If you can accept that things exist in a state of transformation, it will help you overcome the pain of mourning quicker.

If you want to change your life, first change your energy.

Everything is energy and vibration. Yes! You, me, the entire Universe—every tree, brick, and object in our world is composed of energy particles emitting frequencies. Those combined frequencies are people who are magnetizing unique realities to coalesce around them. This is the law of attraction.

The law of attraction is in operation for you even if you do not believe in it or understand how it works. It also does not matter how much you wish for something if your energy frequency is not resonant with it. The Universe doesn't care about our wishes. It can only respond to our frequencies. Like a walking radio tower, the frequency you emit is responsible for the life you have.

If you want something new, change your frequency. To change your frequency, change your thoughts again and again until you've reprogrammed your subconscious mind. The subconscious is in charge.

Just like the moon, we go through phases of emptiness and fullness.

It is all right for you to feel all of your emotions. Society and the people around us might shame us for feeling down, getting overwhelmed, or wanting to rest. But the reality is that we may be in a phase where we need to retreat and be empty. Negating any side of our experience can damage us.

Allow yourself to feel however you genuinely feel. The key to resilience is not to get stuck in one phase of being, but to flow with your emotions and trust that whatever you are going through will pass.

Look at the moon. See how many phases she goes through between empty newness and being whole again. One day, you too, will feel lit up again. Until then, enjoy the beauty of the phase you're in.

Have patience. You can't reap the harvest right after planting seeds.

It takes time to achieve any worthy goal. But waiting for results can make us feel anxious and impatient. Life has a way of testing us by throwing obstacles in our path just to see how committed we really are to our pursuits. If you feel delayed and discouraged, a strategy that may improve your confidence is to look not at the distance between where you are and where you are going, but to look at where you are in comparison to where you were. Seeing how far you've come already can infuse you with hope.

To live resiliently, the most important inner tools to develop are hope, faith, imagination, persistence, and gratitude.

Have faith. Just because you can't see something doesn't mean it doesn't exist.

Faith may be the most important ingredient of accomplishment. In fact, faith is the one condition spoken of as necessary consistently and repeatedly in the Bible. In Matthew 9:29, as Jesus reaches out to restore the sight of some blind men, he says: "According to your faith let it be done to you."

The ability to believe in the invisible truth of your creation before it is manifested guides its creation.

The Universe has a special way of rewarding those who "believe it before seeing it." So, stay in faith. Things could be happening behind the scenes that you cannot yet perceive. Your day, your turn, and your destiny are coming.

The HOW is not up to you.

Feeling discouraged? Every breakthrough that has ever been achieved began just with imagination, a dream, and faith that it could be accomplished. If you have a dream but you don't know how it can be accomplished—perhaps because you don't have the means, contacts, or skills you think are needed, this doesn't mean your objective is out of reach. The HOW of things is not up to you but a higher power that aligns creation with your actions and desires.

In the twentieth century, Sir Edmund Percival Hillary, a New Zealand mountaineer, explorer, and philanthropist, wanted to climb Mount Everest more than anything in the world, even though many people had died trying. He went in 1951 and failed. He went back in 1952 and failed again. Imagine the discouragement he must have felt. But he persisted and went back in 1953. As he stood on top of the mountain all alone, he reflected that he didn't know how he would get there until he did it!

Leap and the bridge will appear!

If you wait until you know how to do something perfectly or for conditions around you to be ideal, you might never accomplish anything. There is always a gap between us and our goals and it can seem as if we're going to fall into a fatal chasm, but the Universe favors the bold. You must leap to cross the divide even if you don't have it all figured out. Intentional action itself causes thing to manifest.

Thomas Edison didn't know how to illuminate the world but he kept working to fulfill his dream of inventing an incandescent light bulb anyhow. He built a bridge step by step, taking leap after leap.

The Wright Brothers were bicycle mechanics in Dayton, Ohio. Though nobody believed they could fly a plane, because they had been trying for years, they saw it as inevitable. They wanted to solve the mystery of flight more than anything in the world, and persisted, but then they did it! Leap by leap, they built a bridge from to the unknown future.

These inventors didn't know how to create their products, but they had the willingness to try and took their leaps in faith. They had faith that if they could conceive "it" in their minds, the "hows" would came to them.

Why would you be any different?

"Everything you thought was drowning you was really teaching you to swim."

ANONYMOUS

Many people will come into your life for a season or a reason.

Not everyone is meant to go the distance with you. You have soul contracts with people who show up in your life. Some of these contracts are short, and once honored, the people involved will leave. There is no point in lamenting the end of any of these relationships. Be grateful it has served you, and accept that you got what you were supposed to.

The one inevitable truth is that after you learn a lesson, another teacher will arrive.

The end of a relationship can hurt, but it also gives you freedom.

When someone tells you they don't love you and plan to leave, let them go, even if it hurts. The person who is meant for you won't need convincing.

Don't be stubborn and try to hold on. This ending has freed you from a situation that was not ideal.

Don't try to bypass the very thing that is here to help you evolve.

There is not one person I know who would willingly choose to suffer; we are designed to seek pleasure and avoid pain at all costs. Even so, going through a storm in life is a universal phenomenon that seems to deliver on a promise like nothing else. None of us is exempt from hurt. Being hurt brings us wisdom.

The Universe will only end a lesson once you have learned what it was supposed to teach you.

The Universe teaches through direct experience. Each lesson is repeated until you master it and the intensity increases as you go along, so you cannot ignore what is happening.

But there's a caveat: Even if you are sure you've learned a certain lesson, the Universe might pitch a curveball at you to test your resolve. If you stubbornly refused to learn a particular lesson, she might schedule a pop quiz to be sure it sticks.

None of us escapes the lessons of Life.

Practicing gratitude doesn't mean turning a blind eye to the ugliness of what you're going through. It is about acknowledging that there's goodness and ease in your life as well as struggle.

Before you ask the Universe for what you want, thank her for what you have.

Challenge yourself, each time you find yourself longing and asking for something, to give thanks for what you already have. A grateful heart attracts abundance.

The goal in finding a partner is not about finding the right person but about *becoming* the right person.

The more you work on becoming all the things you want to attract in a partner the quicker the partner you are looking for will come to you.

The more evolved you become and the more responsibility you take for your life, the higher your odds are of attracting someone equally evolved.

So, spend time nurturing and learning to become the best version of yourself and the rest will follow.

"Every block of stone has a statue inside it, and it is the task of the sculptor to discover it."

MICHELANGELO

Identify what makes you great.

There is greatness in you to be carved out like Michelangelo's sculptures. There is a "sculpture" of virtues in you waiting to be revealed for a purpose. These are faculties and gifts that are uniquely yours. Your mission is to carve them out of raw stone.

What is the thing you do so well that others can't do or say it quite the way you do? What are the values that light a fire in your soul? What words do you have in you that could become a book or song? What ideas do you have that could make life easier for someone? What inventions reside inside you that can transform the world?

Look for your gifts, and when you find them share them with the world. This is your purpose.

The person who grows is the person who makes it a habit to learn from adversity.

Facing fear is one of Life's greatest challenges and the source of Life's greatest rewards.

Fear can stop us from pursuing dreams and goals or tackling new adventures. We can be so comfortable operating in our safety zone that we forget that on the other side of our fear lies treasures.

Make confronting your fears a daily habit. Start with small, uncomfortable fears. As your confidence grows, make your way up to bigger ones.

Purpose comes from pain.

Painful events can be catalysts for massive growth. Life will often use pain as a means to help you find a purpose. The next time you find yourself in one of those dark storms in life, ask, "What could Life be showing me through this pain about my purpose?" Asking the right questions can be empowering.

Your mind can either forge heaven or hell for you by thought alone.

How many stories have you told yourself in your head in the past that caused you to suffer over something you never ultimately experienced? Worry can damage your health. Fighting imaginary battles puts a ton of pressure on the body.

Guaranteed, you'll have many actual battles to fight. It is part of living. So, don't let your mind invent them when you're feeling peaceful.

The next time you panic, take a step back. Ask yourself, "Is this situation real or am I imagining, forecasting, or predicting an outcome that perhaps won't even go the way I think it will?"

Be mindful of the stories you devise in your mind. If you can see they are made up, tell yourself a better story.

The biggest obstacle you'll have to overcome is YOURSELF.

"Ninety percent of your life is working right. Ten percent isn't. If you want to be happy, focus on the 90 percent that works."

OG MANDINO

Forgive yourself for interpreting genuine red-flag warning signs of danger as tests of commitment.

There is no sense shaming and belittling yourself over red flags you have ignored or missed. Guilt and shame are low-frequency emotions that can keep you tied to a person you desperately want to forget. Sometimes, it is difficult to recognize the warning signs if you are too caught up in figuring out ways to make a person love you or change their behavior— or avoid conflict by smoothing things over.

Once you've forgiven yourself, you can learn from the past so you don't relive the same experience.

Life is a roller coaster. You rise, you descend, you laugh, you scream, you hold on tight, you let go, you catch your breath, and then you start the ride all over again.

Failure is never failure if you learn from it.

Change the way you feel about failure. Failure is necessary preparation. It's how Life ensures that you develop the stamina and tenacity for the purpose and path she has planned for you.

The only true failure is not trying.

Stop looking for shortcuts. There aren't any.

Life has no shortcuts. If you want something you must be willing to put in the time, consistency, and discipline to stay on the path. To live an intentional life, you must decide ahead of time for what you want to have and then work diligently to attain your goal.

Resilience in business is about doing the work, day in and day out, especially when you don't want to.

As entertainer Steve Harvey says, "There is no elevator to the top. You must take the stairs.

Surrender your attachment to things.

When you can lay down your need for control (which is an expression of fear), you gain freedom. You free yourself from the pain and the fear and open yourself to the flow of the Universe.

That's EVERYTHING.

When you can look at your life without attachment to things, you gain everything.

Before you leave your bed each morning, express your gratitude for all you have in your life.

When you forget to immerse yourself in gratitude, your energetic blueprint shifts to lack and your life can then be derailed by any annoyance, causing you much stress. But when you wake up in the morning and the first thing you say is, "Thank you, Life, thank you for my place in the world, thank you for my strength to face adversity," you shift your energetic blueprint to abundance.

If you want to be abundant, practice being grateful.

When you experience gratitude in your heart for things and people in your life, your vibration is elevated. As that vibration rises, you tap into the frequency of joyful abundance. You begin to radiate sweet energy that draws loving and grateful things into your life.

When you live with a grateful heart, the Universe conspires to bring you beauty and miracles. Suddenly, the right people serendipitously walk across your path. The answer to a vexing question unexpectedly appears. Opportunities are presented and a whole world of possibility opens up.

If you are looking to the person you are with to "make" you happy, you will forever be dissatisfied.

Happiness is an inside job. It is not the responsibility of your partner to make you happy. The person you choose is there not to supply, but to magnify the happiness you already have.

Many couples break up because one partner, or both, feels the other didn't make them happy. But that is because it is an impossible task.

Only you can do this for yourself.

The real gift of manifestation is not in what material things you attract but in who YOU BECOME in the process.

Be grateful for the closed door.

That opportunity that didn't pan out for you that has you feeling discouraged and disappointed is actually a blessing in disguise. It may be difficult for you to see it in this way right now, but you can trust that the Universe is doing right by you. There are things you cannot see that the Universe knows. She is either saving you from a greater disappointment or preparing you for a greater purpose.

If you focus on problems, you'll attract more problems. If you focus on gratitude, you'll be given more chances to be grateful.

Intimate relationships are the places where you will do most of your emotional healing.

Relationships, especially intimate ones, are soul contracts that come with double-edged swords. Your partner will bring out the best and the worst in you; and sometimes both on the same day. What most people don't know is that these relationships are the most valuable tools we have for discovering all that needs healing in us. Their role is to trigger us to bring to the surface the unhealed feelings we have ignored, denied, and buried. Understanding this will help you be understanding, compassionate, and forgiving when going through disagreements and disappointments with your partner.

Intimate relationships are our best teachers. These are the relationships Life puts on your path to help you grow, heal and evolve.

Life plays no favorites and owes you nothing.

People often feel that Life has dealt them a bad set of cards. But in reality, Life is impartial. What may seem to you like an unfair advantage is simply that some people have become better at mastering the Game of Life. They know what to do with the cards they were dealt. Here are a few things to help you on your journey to best navigate the game of Life.

- Make goals and follow up with action.

- No matter how little you have, do what you can with it.

- Believe you are worthy of the life you are wishing for.

- Expect that things are always working out for you, even if you don't understand how.

- Expand your comfort zone by facing your fears on a daily basis.

- Make mistakes and learn from them.

- Remember that the quality of your thoughts determines what you attract.

- Develop the habit of doing what most people don't like to do.

- Think outside the box.

People are more likely to grow roots in familiar discomfort than grow wings in unknown possibility.

People stay in jobs, relationships, and lifestyles that are mediocre because of a fear of change. Fearing the unknown can be so intense that it overrides any desire to modify something that is bothering them. The lure of familiarity, even the familiarity of discontent and dysfunction, is often more compelling to people than desire and possibility.

This begs the question: What are you putting up with that has you living a life that is second best?

If you are feeling unhappy, unfortunate, or dissatisfied with your life, take inventory of your assets to feel better.

Draw a straight line down the middle of a piece of paper. On the right side of the line, at the top of the page, put the label "My Misfortunes." Below this, list all your grievances, large and small, one by one.

On the left side of the line, at the top of the page, put the label "My Assets." Below this, list all the things in your life that you consider assets. For example, if you woke up this morning, you could put "being alive" under assets. If you could see the sun, put down "the sun." If you awoke with a roof over your head, put "roof" or "shelter" in the asset column. If you could get out of bed and walk, put "walking" under your assets. If you have a family, then list it under your assets.

You get the point.

Sometimes, when we feel like victims, a quick review of our assets can change our mood. This helps us realize how blessed we are.

My Assets   My Misfortunes

Are you looking at your life through the right lens?

Most suffering comes from focusing on things we don't have or that we feel we are being denied and need in order to be happy. This viewpoint represents the scarcity lens.

But earning more money, buying more things, meeting a new partner, or getting a better job will not cure the feeling of having an empty, bottomless hole in your center. If that's what you are ruminating or fantasizing about, it's a clue that you need to swap out the lens you're looking through.

Gratitude is the antidote for lack. Put that lens on your view and you'll notice that Life is brighter.

Your heart may feel broken but it will heal in time so that you can love again. Trust the process.

The heart is an incredibly versatile organ. It gets broken and mends itself. Even if you think you will never love again, your heart will manage to surprise you. It will heal, and then it will help you find a way to love again because love is its natural state.

The best things in Life appear the moment you choose to step into the unknown.

Fear of not knowing where Life is taking us scares us. Anytime we decide to walk into an unknown situation we must face a void of information. Being in this space between the known world and the unknown world can be terrifyingly uncomfortable.

It requires courage and patience to be in the void between what was and what will be. While we are waiting, we tend to make up stories in our heads—predictions that are often more complex than what we actually do experience in the end.

So, the next time you find yourself in such a place, remember that things are sure to be easier to manage than you imagine they will be.

At the lowest points of your life, look for the gift in your pain.

If the walls of your world feel like they are closing in on you, the suggestion to look for a gift in your pain may sound ridiculous or even offensive to you. *"How does one find a gift in something painful?"* you may be wondering. Yet that is precisely what the Universe is asking of you. Your challenge in low moments is to find a seed of bliss—not an easy ask!

Everyone experiences pain, loss, and grief at some point in life. It is what one does with these universal feelings that makes the difference. You can let your circumstances rob you of willpower and cause you to give up, or you can fight to dig yourself out of the hole you're in, and derive some meaning out of it.

Your most humbling and powerful moments come after Life has thrown you down on your knees.

Life does not give you anything that you aren't able to handle. She knows what your soul is made of and the extent of your true strength. Life knows what to put you through in order to get you closer to the destiny meant for you. The adversity you confront can bring out the best in you and make you more resilient than you are today. The best love songs come from broken hearts and the most defining moments of transformation come from being on your knees and looking up at the sky. For this is when you realize, in full humility, how small you are, and yet how powerful for being part of the whole Universe.

Faith and doubt cannot coexist.

Let me ask you something. When you went to bed last night, did you doubt for a second that the morning light would pierce through the darkness of the night? If your answer is no, then you know what faith is. You believed in daybreak without a shadow of a doubt, even though you could not see the sun rising tomorrow yet.

This faith is the same belief, knowingness, and trust you must have in every wonderful dream you have for your life. If you doubt the dream, that is not faith. The minute you doubt it, or question why it is taking too long, you've just disconnected from the divine energy that makes all things possible.

If something is meant for you, then you won't have to beg, fight, or sacrifice for it.

What is meant for you will flow easily to you. If you have to beg, fight, sacrifice, or compromise any part of yourself to get it, then that thing or that person is not divinely intended for you. Learn to recognize the signs of what you need to let go of that you are trying to retain. When something is good for you, it will gravitate to you. That is a prime law of the Universe. Don't waste precious time and effort trying to hold on to things and people that clearly aren't for you.

The biggest mistake you can make is thinking you have more time.

How long of a life you will have is uncertain. Yet most of us live and act as if we have all the time in the world. But consider this: If you knew you had only a few days to live, what would you do differently?

In thinking you have forever to live, you may tend to take Life for granted. Yet going from one breath to the other is a privilege. And there are no guarantees. Open your senses, look around, and appreciate what is there. Live each day as if it were your last. Don't put off doing things you've always wanted to do for another day. Love and express love to those that matter. Don't sweat the small stuff, and make it a habit to stop and smell the roses. Being mindful that your days are limited can help you live to the fullest.

Misfortunes aren't punishments but fuel for the soul.

We are most teachable during moments of affliction because this is when our strengths and talents are forced to the surface. You have levels of resilience, resourcefulness, creativity, humor, and adaptability that you would never have known you possessed unless you needed to use them. But once you've activated a dormant strength, there is no hiding it again. You can continue to use it.

Imagine a stronger version of you in the future looking back at the moment when you rose to meet a challenge that revealed a gift. Future you is likely to be grateful and proud of you for being strong.

Shift the way you look at your misfortunes. They aren't punishments because Life is not out to get you. Let misfortune propel you to lead your best life, ignite your desire, and overcome obstacles.

Relationships: The thing we need most, which is also most difficult.

We thrive when we are in a relationship. Human beings are social animals so we seek connection as part of our survival. Every person seeks love and belonging. It truly is the one thing that we all long for. Yet when we have it, it is often not stress free. Alongside the joy and adventure, there is struggle, conflict, and difficulty. This is because relationships are meant to be our healing path. They come to trigger in us all that needs healing, because the process of friction is where we get to experience a metamorphosis that's impossible to do alone.

Life is not about "mountaintop" moments, but ordinary moments.

Learn to be grateful for the moments that many would consider insignificant. If you look back over your life, you'll recognize that you are most touched and enthusiastic about memories of moments like having a long conversation with a friend, seeing your child take their first steps, dancing in the kitchen with your spouse after dinner. Hearing a joke that makes you laugh uncontrollably.

Big events, like weddings and graduations, are few and far between. What makes up the majority of our lives are micro moments that, in truth, are really the best moments. Listening to rain fall on the roof. Holding hands at the movies. Planting herbs in the garden and then cooking with them later.

The regret of a dying person is not wishing they made more money or achieved more, but wishing they spent more time enjoying the routines of their lives. Learn from the dead and develop the habit of being mindful during ordinary moments. Wake up early to see the sun rise. Make a point to breathe deeply. Savor the developmental milestones of your children. Kiss under the moonlight.

If you look at what you have too little of, you will always want more, but if you look at what you have, you'll always have enough.

If you develop the habit of acknowledging your blessings first thing each morning, especially acknowledging all the things you have taken for granted, you will realize how abundant you are.

The next time you find yourself complaining, take a quick mental inventory of what you have. If your list includes love in your life, health in your body, family to support you, friends to rely on, eyes to see, legs to walk on, a roof over your head, and food on your table, then you are the richest person in the world.

Enough is a matter of gratitude and perspective.

Ninety percent of how your partner triggers you bothers you due to wounds from your past.

Romantic relationships are effective agents for personal growth and healing. Often, it is someone's partner that makes them feel upset, angry, and outraged to the point that they're triggered beyond belief. If your reaction to something your partner has said or done seems out of proportion to the situation, this is a good indication that you are reacting to something from your past that you've been reminded of more than to your partner.

In the absence of awareness, a triggered state can escalate to a dangerous point. So, be sure to ask yourself, *"Is my reaction related to this event or to something deeper that is causing me to feel intensely? Could my subconscious be trying to remind me of something that occurred in my past?"*

Curiosity is good and it can help you deescalate an argument you could regret.

Great relationships don't happen just by chance. They are created by choice.

You may meet someone great by chance, but if you want a great relationship with them you will nurture that love by choice. You make a choice to stay in love with that person. You make a choice to put their happiness at the forefront in your life. And it is a conscious effort you make to choose that same person over and over again each day. If you are feeling estranged from your partner right now, to any degree, remember that you both must choose to create the relationship you want.

Forgiveness is for the one who gives it, not for who receives it.

Many who have been deeply hurt carry a poisonous burden inside, not realizing that the resentment they feel for the one who inflicted pain on them is what keeps them tied to this person they so desperately want to forget.

Beware of the anger you hold for those who wronged you. It only affects one person—YOU! If you wish to move on, forgive. If you wish to live with a light heart, forgive. This is not excusing what another person did, but liberation for your soul.

Forgiveness is a gift you give to yourself.

A key to freedom is knowing that you've got the power to choose what to accept and what to let go.

Nobody has more power to hurt you than you. We build our own mental and emotional prisons by holding on to resentment, anger, guilt, and shame. Get in the habit of letting go regularly so you can travel lighter through this wondrous journey that is Life. You possess the key to unlock your prison cell.

Truths to consider:

- Remarkable achievements are attained by taking steady, incremental action.

- Words carry power. With them, we can heal and destroy on the same day.

- There is no such thing as failure if you keep trying and continue learning.

- There is nothing more powerful than the practice of gratitude.

- The quickest way out of pain is by helping others.

- Learn from the past and be curious, hopeful, and pragmatic about the future.

- Accept that not all things will turn out the way you want and that's OK.

- A life well lived requires purpose. Exist for something bigger than yourself.

When times are bad, pray.
When times are good, pray.

It is natural to pray for divine help and guidance in moments of crisis and need. Seldom, however, do we remember to say a prayer of thanks when things are working out for us. We forget to honor our joy and abundance and give credit to the divine.

When times are good, say "Thank you."

When times are bad, say "Thank you for giving me strength, resilience, and wisdom."

The secret to an abundant, joyful life is to say thank you constantly to the Universe for everything. When you express gratitude, the vibration of it is mirrored back to you. You get more of the same.

"Big doors swing on little hinges."

W. CLEMENT STONE

Never underestimate the power of the little things.

The little moments in Life, the small gestures of kindness and friendship, the small steps in the right direction, the ideas for little improvements—these are what eventually amount to big transformations and great accomplishments. Big victories are won through consistent, steady actions. Great loves are built in the micro-moments of care and concern.

Expectations are prophecies.

You get what you expect from Life. There is a real correlation between what we believe we deserve, or are worthy of having, and our potential and the ultimate quality of our lives. Hence, the adage "God meets us at the level of our expectations."

Your expectations of Life and your personal value and capabilities act as prophecies. If you expect to experience blessings, breakthroughs, and healing then that is precisely what you'll experience. Be mindful of the bars you are setting to jump.

People can't change people.

If you are in a situation of hoping to help someone change poor behavior, and doing all you can, stop. People cannot change people . . . unless they want to change themselves. All the love in the world won't help a person who doesn't want to change, and that is not your job nor the purpose of your journey. Real change can only come when a person acknowledges their need for change and diligently does the work to become who they want to be.

Don't think for a second that your love can be enough to make anyone else do something. You will be hurt and disappointed. Accept the person as they are or move on. Potential is NOT a reason or indication of who the person decides to be.

Suffering cannot dwell in the landscape of a grateful heart.

When you are grateful, it is almost impossible to feel unhappy or upset. When your heart is swollen with gratitude, you cannot hold a grudge. Only one emotion can prevail at any given moment. Choose to look for the positive in the people around you. There are two sides to every coin, but if you favor the positive in all your encounters, your heart will naturally overflow with peace and gratitude.

You change your life the minute you realize that all you need is already within you. The love you seek, the abundance you aspire to, the health you wish for are made possible when you change your energetic frequency. When you live as if YOU ARE already those things, ahead of these events, you will have the life of your dreams.

Things that can help you become more resilient:

- Understanding you are not alone. A divine force guides and protects you at all times.

- It is your birthright to ask God/the Universe/ Life for help.

- What you perceive as a loss or a denial of your requests in the moment may be an occasion of divine protection.

- The life you have is a consequence of your habits, beliefs, thoughts, and emotions. If you are looking for someone to blame for a poor consequence, look in the mirror. If you are looking for someone to save you, look in the mirror.

- Hold no one else responsible for your happiness.

- Embrace failure, as it is a steppingstone bringing you closer to any goal.

To succeed, it is ideal to focus on only one step at time.

If you look at a mountain in its entirety, it will always seem impossible to climb. If you know the climb is 20,000 steps long, your brain will give you a hundred reasons why you won't make it. This is the main reason many people fail to achieve their goals. As they look at the end of the road or focus on the entire trajectory of the path up and down, the task seems so daunting that they quit before they even try. The mountain seems *insurmountable.*

When you stand in front of your mountain (as it may be) and focus only on taking the first step, then the second step, then the third, taking it one step at a time without contemplating the 19,997 steps still to come, you will soon begin to make achieve that which was once an impossibility in your mind.

Never underestimate the power of tackling what is right in front of you. This is a key to resilience.

You don't have to have everything figured out to begin or continue.

In the most difficult times of my life, I have leaned on the belief that I am not alone. And I have thanked the Universe in advance for carrying me through moments when I would not be able to stand on my own two legs. There is something comforting and powerful when you trust that a divine force is protecting you and knows the path.

When in doubt, remember that you don't have to have it all figured out. Trust that the Universe will find the best resolution, one for the benefit of all.

The best healers in the world are:

- Gratitude.
- Sunshine.
- Sleep.
- Exercise.
- A healthy diet.
- Love.
- Human connection.
- Purpose.

If you have a dream, protect it.

Be mindful of whom you share your dreams with. People, including those you love, will sometimes try to discourage you when they hear about them. Not out of malice, but because, in their minds, your dreams are out of reach and they don't want you to be disappointed or fail and need their assistance.

The most difficult thing in the world is to hear people you love, and whose support you long for, tell you a hundred reasons why your dream is not going to happen. They will tell you that you don't have the economic means, the knowledge, the contacts, or the know-how to make a go of it.

Never let others' opinions rob you of your dreams. Be aware of the dream-killers. It is usually not that they want to hurt you—though some may feel envy. It is usually that they don't understand the creative principle that you know. One that great doers in history have always known.

What is that? That the place where we create from doesn't care that we don't know how to do it yet.

Choose your battles carefully.

The greatest victory is that which requires no battle. In *The Art of War,* Sun Tzu shared this principle, which is just as true today as it was in antiquity. And just as true in our personal and business lives as it is in times of actual warfare between nations. If you "go to battle" with your children, your partner, or a colleague, then that is not a victory for anyone.

Every time you win an argument at the expense of the dignity of another, it's not a win. Each time a person is forced to concede to you by threat or guilt, you lose. You may think you have won, and perhaps you may win that argument or concession, but in the end, you'll lose the "war." Try instead to persuade them to concede of their own accord.

Adopt a strategy of developing win-win scenarios. Aim to meet in the middle between points of view so that everyone involved in a conflict walks away feeling they've won something. If you can do this, you will have peace in your family and career.

Who would you rather become?

There's a difference between a victim and a doer.

The victim is a person who feels Life is somehow out to get them, that circumstances are happening *TO* them. They blame their current state of affairs on the unfairness of Life and things beyond their control. As a victim, this person seeks a savior and is always at the mercy of others. Most of us have adopted this perspective at some point.

The doer is a person who takes responsibility for their current state of affairs and believes that Life is happening THROUGH them. Control is an intrinsic part of their consciousness. As a doer, they see it as their role to make things happen by altering their circumstances. They tend to push against Life, and can fall into a pattern of hyper vigilance and force.

A person who is in the flow of Life, by comparison, recognizes their gifts and takes responsibility for the results manifesting in their life, but they feel little need for control. They believe that Life flows through them and circumstances are happening FOR them for a reason. The mystical is an intrinsic part of their consciousness. They see the invisible hand of a greater power at work, conspiring with them, and guiding them to their highest destiny.

You have a choice of two lenses through which to look at Life.

You can look at your life through narrow or wide lenses, but not both simultaneously. With the narrow lenses, you can focus on things you don't like or that are not working well for you.

 With the wide lenses you see all. You can see those same things, but you also see the good. You can choose to focus on things that you like or that are working well.

Which lenses are you using to navigate your existence?

Even when times are tough, you will be more resilient if you don't lose sight of the good.

The Universe will respect your free will even to your own detriment.

There is a dichotomy between asking God/Life/ the Universe for help and how we behave that sabotages the results we have requested. This is why some people pray and get poor results.

Unless you get out of your own way, your prayer may never be answered. Why? Because the Universe will never violate your free will. She will send you signs about what to do and people to alert you to the best choices, and set up conditions that can move you forward, but she will respect your right to choose your path to fulfill your destiny.

You have nothing to prove.

People spend precious energy proving their worthiness to others. Frankly, this can be exhausting. If you frequently find yourself looking for the approval of your boss, your spouse, or your friends, and hoping this will make you feel worthy or important, then you have forgotten the simple truth: You have nothing to prove.

You've already won the biggest battle in Life: Out of millions of your father's sperm, you were the one who won the race to impregnate your mother. Scientists have calculated the odds of you being born as being as remote as one in 400 trillion. That means, your existence is literally miraculous.

What better recognition of worthiness could you possibly need after that?

Your mind is more obedient than you imagine.

Your mind's "job" is to find evidence to support what you tell it. If you tell it (mentally) that Life is hard, difficult, unfair, stressful, and painful, then those are precisely the types of situations that your mind will look to put you in or create for you. It will direct you to do things and surround you with people that support your hypothesis.

The reality is that Life isn't any particular way. If you want to change what you experience, then you must start by changing what you tell your mind. Plain and simple.

There will never be a perfect time to start, so you might as well start now.

If you wait for situations to be perfect in order to start, you will never get going. The time to start that new business you've been dreaming of is now. The time to start that eating plan you've intended to adopt is today. The time to start expressing love is now. The cemetery is full of people who took their dreams to the grave waiting for perfect conditions. Your story can be different from theirs!

You can talk yourself into or out of your dreams.

Yes, you are that powerful!

When feeling loss or sorrow, shift your focus. Never mind what you lost or what this person or that event took from you. Pay attention to the lessons and the wisdom that you gained because of it.

There really is no more powerful story than your own.

No matter how ordinary you may think your life is, if you tell your story to someone else, describing the things you've overcome and experienced, the lessons you've learned, the adventures you've taken, things you've seen, and amazing and weird characters who have crossed your path, you will realize how amazing and unique your life has been so far. Don't underestimate your journey.

You have a reservoir of wisdom in your mind that can impact the world positively. Don't look outside yourself to discern what kind of contribution to make, because everything you need to make this decision is already within you.

Light shines through cracks.

Kintsugi is the Japanese art of putting broken pottery pieces back together and sealing the repair with lacquer dusted with gold, silver, or platinum. This tradition of conservation is built on the philosophy that embracing flaws and imperfections creates stronger, more interesting pieces of art.

The same is true for us. When we feel damaged, we mend our "damage" by transcending the past. Every setback, every hurt, serves to crack you open, so the light of wisdom and love can shine through you. You are not permanently damaged or ruined by hardship; you're a beautiful, mended work of art with a storied history that makes you valuable.

CREDITS

Og Mandino. *Og Mandino's University of Success: The Greatest Self-Help Author in the World Presents the Ultimate Success Book* (New York: Bantam Books, 1982): p. 44.

Joel Osteen. *Keep Your Walls Up Podcast* (2019).

Joe Dispenza in an Interview with Tom Bilyeu from Impact Theory. "Learn How to Control Your Mind (Use This to Brainwash Yourself)," Fearless Soul Channel, YouTube.com.

Frank Lewis Dyer. *Edison: His Life and Inventions, volume 2* (1910).

George F. Pentecost. *The Angel in the Marble, and Other Papers* (1883).

Steve Harvey. "There Is No Elevator to the Top," Official Steve Harvey Channel, YouTube.com (June 19, 2019).

Mel Robbins. "How to Stop Screwing Yourself Over," TEDx Talks Channel, YouTube.com (June 11, 2011).

COPYRIGHT NOTICE

DreamCatcher Print / Waleuska Lazo
Hollywood, Florida
WaleuskaLazo.com

Library of Congress Control Number 2023909296

ISBN 978-1-7327431-8-2 (paperback)
ISBN 978-1-7327431-9-9 (kindle ebook)

RESOURCES

Come to my website:

WaleuskaLazo.com

Join me on the social networks:

FACEBOOK
https://facebook.com/waleuskalazoauthor

INSTAGRAM
https://www.instagram.com/
waleuskalazo

YOUTUBE
https://www.youtube.com/waleuskalazo

LINKEDIN
https://www.linkedin.com/in/
waleuska-lazo-337623141/de

TWITTER
https://twitter.com/waleuskalazo

Hire me as a speaker:

wlazo@WaleuskaLazo.com

ABOUT THE AUTHOR

WALEUSKA LAZO is an author and the creator of FMTG: The 28-Day Five Minutes to Gratitude Transformational Course. Her books include *The Gratitude Blueprint, The Best Worst Thing That Happened to Me, Confessions from a Mom to Her Child,* and *The Gift of Bravery.* She enjoys helping people transform their pain into wisdom, traveling the world, and spending time with her daughters.

Manufactured by Amazon.ca
Bolton, ON